Alto Saxophone Student

by Fred Weber and Major Herman Vincent

To The Student

This book, with the aid of a good teacher, is designed to help you become an excellent player on your instrument in a most enjoyable manner. It will take a reasonable amount of work and CAREFUL practice on your part. If you do this, learning to play should be a valuable and pleasant experience.

To The Teacher

The Belwin "Student Instrumental Course" is the first and only complete course for private instruction of all band instruments. Like instruments may be taught in classes. Cornets, trombones, baritones and basses may be taught together. The course is designed to give the student a sound musical background and at the same time provide for the highest degree of interest and motivation. The entire course is correlated to the band oriented sequence.

To make the course both authoritative and practical, most books are co-authored by a national authority on each instrument in collaboration with Fred Weber, perhaps the most widely-known and accepted authority at the student level.

The Belwin "Student Instrumental Course" has three levels: elementary, intermediate, and advanced intermediate. Each level consists of a method and three correlating supplementary books. In addition, a duet book is available for Flute, B♭ Clarinet, E♭ Alto Sax, B♭ Cornet and Trombone. The chart below shows the correlating books available with each part.

The Belwin "STUDENT INSTRUMENTAL COURSE" A course for individual and class instruction of LIKE instruments, at three levels, for all band instruments.

EACH BOOK IS COMPLETE IN ITSELF BUT ALL BOOKS ARE CORRELATED WITH EACH OTHER

METHOD
"The Alto Saxophone Student"
For individual
or
class instruction.

ALTHOUGH EACH BOOK CAN BE USED SEPARATELY, IDEALLY, ALL SUPPLEMENTARY BOOKS SHOULD BE USED AS COMPANION BOOKS WITH THE METHOD

STUDIES AND MELODIOUS ETUDES	TUNES FOR TECHNIC	THE ALTO SAXOPHONE SOLOIST	DUETS FOR STUDENTS
Supplementary scales, warm-up and technical drills, musicianship studies and melody-like studies.	Technical type melodies, variations, and "famous passages" from musical literature — for the development of technical dexterity.	Interesting and playable graded easy solo arrangements of famous and well-liked melodies. Also contains 2 Duets, and 1 Trio. Easy piano accompaniments.	Easy duet arrangements of familiar melodies for early ensemble experience. Available for: Flute B♭ Clarinet Alto Sax B♭ Cornet Trombone

Elementary Fingering Chart
How To Read The Chart

● – Indicates hole closed or keys to be pressed.

○ – Indicates hole open.

When a number is given, refer to the picture of the Saxophone for additional key or keys to be pressed.

When two ways to finger a note are given, the first way is the one most often used. The second fingering is for use in special situations.

When two notes are given together (F♯ and G♭) they are the same tone and, of course, played the same way.

Only those fingerings necessary in the Elementary Phase of Saxophone playing are given.

B.I.C.131

Getting Started

How to hold

the

SAXOPHONE

STUDY PHOTOS ABOVE FOR PROPER POSITION AND HOW TO HOLD THE INSTRUMENT.

FOLLOW YOUR TEACHER'S INSTRUCTIONS ON HOW TO PRODUCE A TONE ON THE SAX.

THE SUGGESTIONS BELOW MAY BE HELPFUL.

- Experiment to find the right amount of mouthpiece to put in the mouth. Usually the teeth touch the mouthpiece about ½" from the tip (end).

- There should be a slight amount of the red part of the lip (about ¼") between the teeth and the reed.

- Keep corners of mouth tight. Do not let your cheeks "puff out".

- Blow a reasonable amount of air into the sax.

- A moderate amount of jaw and lip pressure is best.

- Use a reed of moderate strength.

- Adjust strap so you can always sit correctly and bring the saxophone to its proper position. *DO NOT BEND OVER, OR REACH OUT FOR THE SAXOPHONE.*

OTHER VALUABLE SUGGESTIONS.

(1)   Playing with good tone and in tune are two of the most important aspects of playing, and are two of the most difficult to master. You must have a good instrument (in good condition), with a good mouthpiece and reed.

(2)   Count at all times — — — while practicing at home, in lessons, or in band.

(3)   Hold the instrument in the correct position, at all times. Sit erectly and be sure the hands, arms and fingers are all in the correct positions. Without correct position none of the other important habits can be mastered properly.

(4)   Keep your instrument clean at all times, especially the mouthpiece.

(5)   Always keep relaxed, especially the fingers, when playing.

(6)   *A HALF HOUR OF CAREFUL, THOUGHTFUL PRACTICE IS WORTH MANY HOURS OF CARELESS PRACTICE.*

Lesson 1

Reading Music

You should know the following rudiments before starting to play:

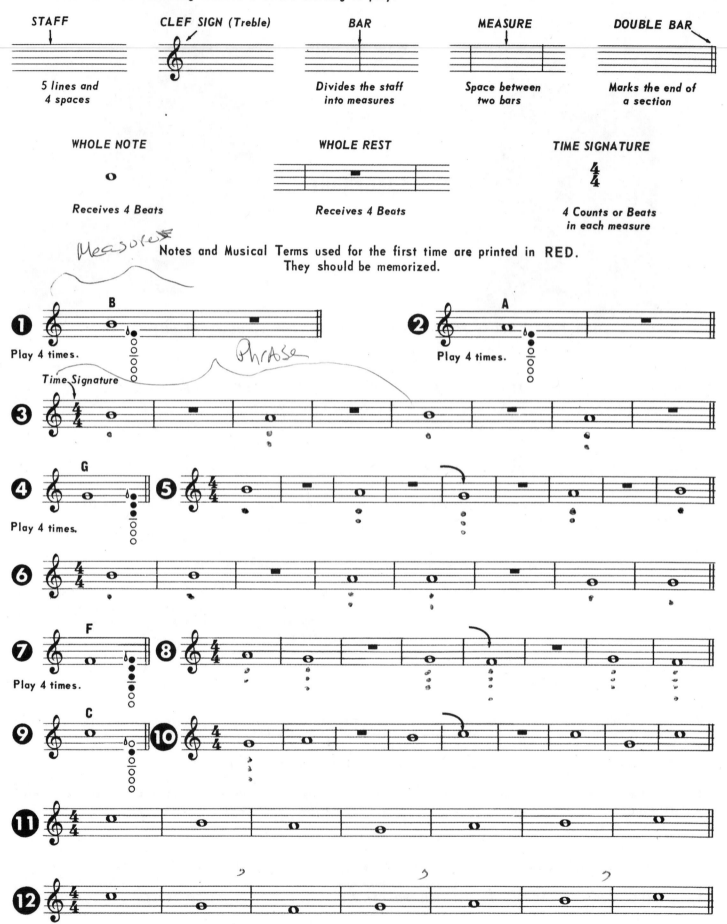

STAFF — 5 lines and 4 spaces

CLEF SIGN (Treble)

BAR — Divides the staff into measures

MEASURE — Space between two bars

DOUBLE BAR — Marks the end of a section

WHOLE NOTE — Receives 4 Beats

WHOLE REST — Receives 4 Beats

TIME SIGNATURE — 4/4 — 4 Counts or Beats in each measure

Notes and Musical Terms used for the first time are printed in RED.
They should be memorized.

Lesson 2

QUARTER NOTE
1 count.

BREATH MARK - *means to breathe*

For the first few pages, <u>name</u> and <u>finger</u> the notes before you play each line.

QUARTER REST
1 count.

Write counting under notes.

Count 1 2 3 4   1 2 3 4   1

Merrily We Roll Along

Suggestion: Do these things before playing this melody:
1. Sing using the words;   2. Sing using letter names of notes and silently finger the notes;
3. Play on your Sax.

Mer - ri - ly we roll a - long   etc.

Put the NUMBER of the LINE or SPACE the note is on, in the square and write below whether the note is on a line or space.

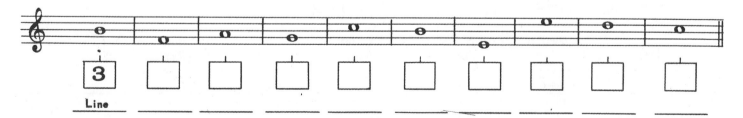

3
Line

Lesson 3

PUT THE FOLLOWING ON THE STAFF:

Whole Note	Quarter Note	A Time Signature	Quarter Rest	Half Note	Half Rest	Tie two Notes

Lesson 4

DOTTED HALF NOTE
Gets 3 counts.

C stands for Common time and is the same as 4/4 time.

Repeat Dots — Repeat the line

See note below
* * — means use alternate fingering.

Repeat line

← Alternate fingering for C.

Counting Fun
Write counting under notes, then play.

1 2 3 4 etc.

A-Tiskit A-Taskit

PICK-UP NOTE (Ask your teacher to explain.)

Play 1st time only. Play 2nd time only.

Count→ 4 1 2 3 4 etc.

2nd time

Lightly Row
Duet

1st Part (Student)

2nd Part (Teacher)

Also F#

ALTERNATE FINGERINGS

Some notes can be fingered more than one way. We call these additional fingerings, *Alternate Fingerings* Sometimes it is easier or necessary to use the alternate fingerings depending on which notes come before and after. We learn to use these alternate fingerings now because they must be used later when we learn to play faster. Teachers have different ideas on when these alternate fingerings should be learned. Ask your teacher how he wants you to finger third space C when it comes between two B's.

REVIEW OF NOTES: ❶ Name notes. ❷ Mark fingering. ❸ Play on Sax.

Lesson 5

You are now ready to begin the companion books, STUDIES AND MELODIOUS ETUDES and TUNES FOR TECHNIC, correlated with the Method as part of the BELWIN STUDENT INSTRUMENTAL COURSE.

The Cuckoo Waltz

Octaves

Counting Fun

Peter, Peter

Counting Duet

❶ Put names of notes in squares above staff. ❷ Fill in correct fingering.
The first one is a sample.

Lesson 6

The Old Gray Goose

Counting Fun

A Sharp (♯) makes a tone sound ½ step higher. A Natural (♮) merely cancels a sharp (or flat). Any note not sharped (or flatted) is a natural. We only use the natural sign (♮) when we want to remove or cancel a sharp or flat.

College Melody

Down In The Valley
Duet

Write a T below the ties and an S below the slurs.

Lesson 7

You are now ready to begin the companion books, STUDIES AND MELODIOUS ETUDES and TUNES FOR TECHNIC, correlated with the Method as part of the BELWIN STUDENT INSTRUMENTAL COURSE.

The Mouse Ran Up the Clock

Play 2 times. The first time play entire melody - second time, omit notes marked ★ and substitute a quarter rest.

♦ KEY SIGNATURE - means all Fs are played F♯. (See note below.)

To remind you the note is F♯. See Key Signature.

Also F♯

Crazy Counting

What tune is this line based on?

Symphony Theme

DVORAK

2nd time

March Trio

2/4 TIME - 2 counts in each measure.

See page 11 for explanation of flat in signature.

❶ Put notes called for on the staff. ❷ Mark fingering.   Use only notes you have learned.

| B | High A | A | High G | G | C | High F♯ | F♯ | High F | F | E | D |

♦ *Sometimes it is necessary to place a sharp at the beginning of a line. This avoids the necessity of placing a sharp in front of each F. When there is a sharp in the signature it is always F♯ and the Key is G. It is in the Key of G because the melody, or study, is based on the scale of G. When F♯ is in the Key Signature, both High and Low F are played F♯.*

Until No. 5 on this page there has been no Key Signature. When there is no Key Signature the piece is in the Key of C.

Lesson 8

Comparing C And ¢ Time

Lesson 9

Melody Fun

Play 3 times. The first time play the entire melody. 2nd time - omit all notes marked with ② and substitute a rest. 3rd time - omit all notes marked ② and ③ and substitute quarter rests.

Gypsy Love Song

Duet

Onward Christian Soldiers

Slowly and majestically - well accented

① See bottom of page.

Open (No Fingering)

② See below.

③ See below.   ④ See below.

Although ♩. and ♪♪ rhythms haven't been introduced in the Method as yet, this solo is otherwise so playable and enjoyable, we decided to use it at this time. With a little explanation from the teacher, it should give very little trouble. Exposure to these new rhythms at this time will be helpful when they are introduced later in the Method. Teachers who prefer may substitute the measures below for the proper measures in the solo.

These measures may be substituted for measures above - as marked.

Lesson 10

You are now ready for DUETS FOR STUDENTS, a book of easy duet arrangements of familiar melodies coordinated with the BELWIN STUDENT INSTRUMENTAL COURSE.

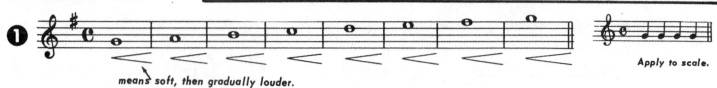

means soft, then gradually louder.

Apply to scale.

Write counting under notes, then play.

Goodnight Ladies

Counting Fun

Caisson March

Count {
C → 3 4   1 2 3 4   1 etc.
¢ → 2   +   1 + 2   +   1 etc.
}

Write the counting under the measures below.

Lesson 11

1 Practice both octaves.

2

3

4

Left Hand - 1st finger on both pearl keys.

5

Octaves

6

Etude in F

7

Grandfathers Clock

8

Fine

D.C. al Fine

Famous March Theme

9

Put in the bar lines.

Lesson 12

You are now ready to play solos from THE ALTO SAXOPHONE SOLOIST, a book of solos with Piano Ac - companiments correlated with the Method as part of the BELWIN STUDENT INSTRUMENTAL COURSE.

Thirds

1

Try various articulations (tonguing and slurring combinations) on Lines 1, 2 and 3.

Thirds

2

Thirds

3

Chromatic Waltz

4

Check with your teacher about alternate fingering for F#. Most teachers prefer the chromatic F# fingering.

Yankee Doodle Variation

This is an ACCENT MARK and means to accent or make this note stand out.

5

Bicycle Built for Two

6

Double Note Duet

7

Melody

Harmony

Lesson 13

Lesson 14

is intended to picture a well played tone that doesn't wave and stays on exactly the same pitch.

1

AVOID tones of the type pictured below.

ⓐ A "Scooped" attack.   ⓑ A wavy Tone.   ⓒ Attack not clean.   ⓓ A Tone that goes flat.   ⓔ (1) Accented tongue release. (2) Over-accented attack.

Wrong   Wrong   Wrong   Wrong   Wrong

(1)
(2)

D Scale

2

3

4

Chromatic Etude

5

This Old Man

6

When The Saints Go Marching In

7

Count 2 3 4   1   etc.
Count + 2 +   1   etc.

Lesson 15

1 means gradually softer - Tone must be steady and smooth.

2 Low C

3 What Key is this? _____
Also play slurred.

4 *alternate fingering

Crazy Counting

5

Birthday Greetings

6

Melody In F

7

Lesson 16

Review Of Keys

Lesson 17

EIGHTH REST - Same time value as Eighth Note (♪).   Staccato — means short or separated.

Notes with a dot over or under them (♩) are played Staccato. This means to play them short and light. The notes should be separated with a slight rest between each note depending on the character of the piece.

Andante From The Surprise Symphony

HAYDN

High B

C Scale (2 Octaves)

High C

Scale Etude

To A Wild Rose

MacDOWELL

Slowly with expression

Lesson 18

Notes with an Accent Mark ($\geq$) over or under them are emphasized and played with extra force. In a series they are usually separated with slight rests between each note.

Lesson 19

Tone must be steady and smooth.

①

Apply these *PATTERNS*
to Scale Above

(a)   (b)

②

Etude

③

Merry Widow Waltz

LEHAR

④

In the measures below is the second note HIGHER: LOWER: or the SAME as the first note?   Use H, L, and S.

 H

Sample

Lesson 20

Apply these PATTERNS to Scale Above

(a) (b) (c) Legato Mark — See Below (d) *ff mf p*

Rainbow Theme

Many times in music certain groups of notes go together and should be played in the same breath. These notes are often indicated by a long curved line similar to a slur. This is called a phrase. A Phrase might be thought of as a musical sentence. The notes may be tongued softly.

alternate fingering

Can Can

Work out slowly, then try for speed.

Give Full Count

A short line under or over a note (♩) means to play the note legato or very smoothly and with a very soft tongue stroke. It might be thought of as the opposite of staccato. There is no separation of notes.

Lesson 21

Etude In D

Dotted Quarter Notes

DOTTED QUARTER NOTE

The author suggests that you tap twice on the dotted quarter notes (♩.). The eighth note (♪) comes midway between the 2nd and 3rd taps.

America

p ← Stands for PIANO and means play softly

Etude

Home On The Range

f ← Stands for FORTE and means play loudly

Lesson 22

1 Play staccato 1st time and legato 2nd time.   etc.

2 High Bb

3

4

Chromatic Scale

Use alternate fingering.

5

The Octave Waltz

6

Etude In F

7

College Song

8

mp — Stands for MEZZO PIANO and means to play moderately soft

Michael Row The Boat

9

Count 3 4 1

mf — Stands for MEZZO FORTE and means to play moderately loud

Lesson 23

♦KEY SIGNATURE - See below.

Counting Fun **Billy Boy**

Count 2 + 1

Yankee Doodle Boy

ff ← Stands for **FORTISSIMO** and means to play very loud

Count 1 + 2 + 1 + 2 + 1

♦When there are two flats in the signature, the second flat is always Eb. This means the piece is based on the Bb Scale and all Bs and Es are flatted.

Lesson 24

Etude In C

Play in a light, separated, manner.

Review Etude

Under The Double Eagle

Trio

Count 2 1

Lesson 25

The name of this KEY is_____?

Thirds

① Practice the first six lines using various combinations of tonguing and slurring: ♩♩♩♩ | ♩♩♩♩ | ♩♩♩♩ | ♩♩♩♩ | etc.

The name of this KEY is_____?

②

The name of this KEY is_____?

Thirds

③

The name of this KEY is_____?

Thirds

④

The name of this KEY is_____?

Thirds
*

⑤

Chromatic Review

⑥ ⑦

same

⑧ ⑨
*

⑩ ⑪
same

⑫ ⑬

⑭
same

Articulation Review

⑮

> > > >

Lesson 26

③⁸ TIME - 3 counts to each measure.

♪ – 1 Count;   ♩ – 2 Counts;   ♩. – 3 Counts.

The Man On The Flying Trapeze

pp → Stands for PIANISSIMO and means to play very softly

Sweet Betsy From Pike Same Tempo (♪ gets one count)

Don't Stop

Lesson 27

Lesson 28

My Wild Irish Rose

Over The Waves

Fun with Counting

Lesson 29

If the foot-tapping method of counting is used make sure the foot comes UP (Up beat) in EXACTLY the MIDDLE of the BEAT.

1	⟶	♩	– receives 1 Count
2	⟶	♫	– receive 1 Count
4	⟶	♬	– receive 1 Count

Sixteenth Notes

Count 1 + 2 + 1

Variation

Won't You Come Home Bill Bailey

Lesson 30

Theme From *The Opera, William Tell*

Lesson 31

Theme From Moment Musical

SCHUBERT

LEGATO STUDY — Play slowly in a broad and sustained manner.

American Patrol

Lesson 32

KEY SIGNATURE - See below.

Review Etude

Trepak

TSCHAIKOWSKY

When we have three sharps in the Key Signature, they are always F#, C# and G#. The Key is A. It means the piece is based on the Scale of A and all Fs, Cs and Gs are sharped.

Lesson 33

Dinah

Nocturne

Play slowly in a legato, songlike manner.

MENDELSSOHN

The long curved line joining several measures is a *Phrase Mark* and means that all of the notes within the curved line are played in a single breath. It can be compared to a sentence in a paragraph. The notes may be tongued smoothly.

Rondo

HAYDN

Basic Technic

Scales

Scales In Thirds

Basic Technic

Practice as assigned by your Teacher

The Patterns below provide for unlimited scale practice in the 7 most common band keys.
FOLLOW THESE INSTRUCTIONS.

Start with ANY line and play through the entire pattern without stopping. Return to the STARTING LINE and play to where the END is marked. You must keep the KEY SIGNATURE of the STARTING LINE THROUGHOUT the entire pattern.

Same as C♯ – See beginning of line

Speed Test

Name the notes. Work for speed. The test should be completed in 1 minute and 30 seconds or less.

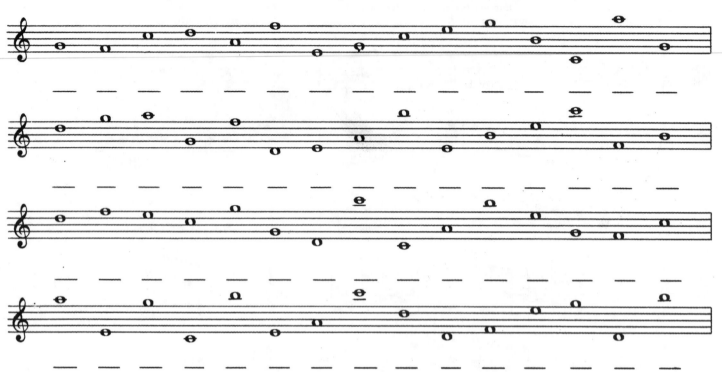

Home Practice Record

Week	Mon.	Tues.	Wed.	Thurs.	Fri.	Sat.	Total	Parent's Signature	Week	Mon.	Tues.	Wed.	Thurs.	Fri.	Sat.	Total	Parent's Signature
1									21								
2									22								
3									23								
4									24								
5									25								
6									26								
7									27								
8									28								
9									29								
10									30								
11									31								
12									32								
13									33								
14									34								
15									35								
16									36								
17									37								
18									38								
19									39								
20									40								